Why Is This Festival Special?

Id-ul-Fitr

Jillian Powell

W
FRANKLIN WATTS
LONDON • SYDNEY

This edition 2009

Franklin Watts
338 Euston Road
London NW1 3BH

Franklin Watts Australia
Level 17/207 Kent Street
Sydney NSW 2000

Copyright © Franklin Watts 2005

Series editor: Sarah Peutrill
Art director: Jonathan Hair
Picture researcher: Diana Morris
Design: Ian Thompson
Consultant: Ghulam Sarwar, Director of The
Muslim Education Trust, London

A CIP catalogue record for this book is available
from the British Library

ISBN: 978 0 7496 9015 1
Dewey classification number: 297.3'6

Printed in Malaysia

Picture credits: Muhammed Bazuki/Reuters/Corbis:
7, 10b. Marco Brivio/Alamy: 17t. Juliet Highet/Ark
Religion: 24. Image Works/Topfoto: 21t. Ali
Jarekji/Reuters/Corbis: 8. C. Ray Moller/Franklin
Watts: cover b, 9b, 13t, 17b, 18t, 19t, 20t, 21b.
Rennie/Ark Religion: 16. Helene Rogers/Ark
Religion: 9, 19b, 20b, 25t. Roshan
Sharma/Photographers Direct: front cover t, 10c.
World Religions Picture Library: 3, 6, 12, 13b, 15t,
15b, 18b, 22, 23t, 23b, 25b, 26, 27t, 27b. A.
Zerbaigan/Topfoto: 11.

Every attempt has been made to clear copyright.
Should there be any inadvertent omission please
apply to the publisher for rectification.

Franklin Watts is a division of Hachette Children's
Books, an Hachette UK company.
www.hachette.co.uk

Note: When Muslims say the name of one of the prophets, they always say afterwards 'Peace Be Upon Him', which is shown in this book as 'pbuh'.

Contents

A happy festival

Id-ul-Fitr is a Muslim festival. Muslims are people who follow a religion called Islam. They believe in one God, called Allah.

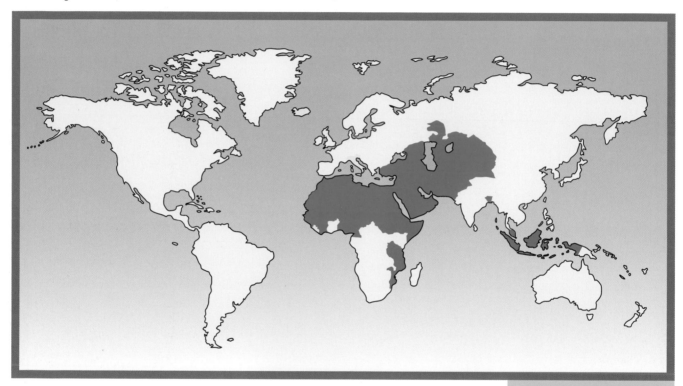

Muslims study their holy book, the Qur'an and try to live their lives doing what Allah wants them to do.

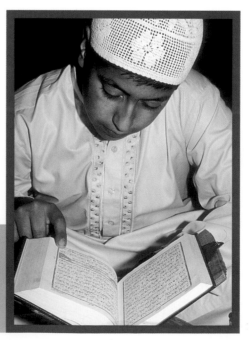

Islam is the main religion of over 60 countries. The countries where more than half of the people are Muslim are shown in green.

In Muslim countries Muslim children read the Qur'an in school, as well as at home.

Id-ul-Fitr (often called just Id) celebrates the end of Ramadan, a holy month when most Muslims fast. Fasting means they do not eat, drink, or smoke in the daytime.

Id is a time for giving thanks to Allah and celebrating with family and friends, and also a time for making others happy.

Id-ul-Fitr is celebrated for one day.

" At the start of Id, we all wish each other 'Id Mubarak' which means Happy Festival. "
Shaheen, aged 10

A young Malaysian girl plays with a sparkler on the eve of the Id celebrations.

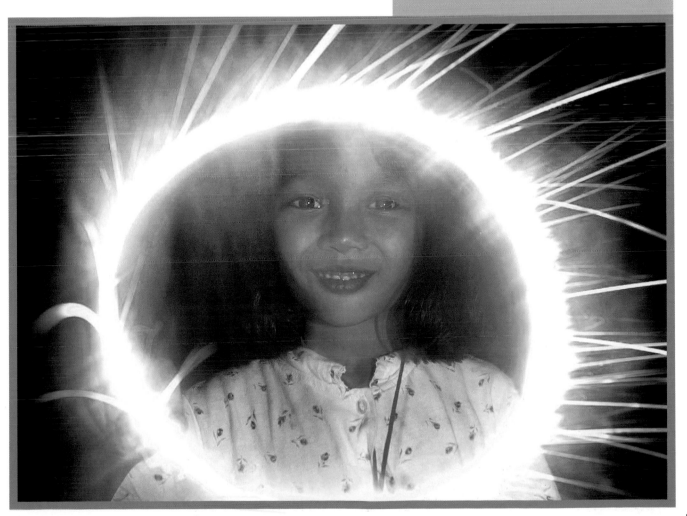

Ramadan

Ramadan is a time for fasting.

Ramadan is the ninth month in the Islamic calendar (see page 29). It is a very holy month. It begins when the new moon is seen.

During Ramadan, Muslims go without food and water all day. They only eat before dawn, and after sunset.

The new moon is when the moon first appears as a crescent in the sky.

A Muslim family pray before sharing a meal together before dawn.

Fasting is important for Muslims. It helps them to show that they are thinking about Allah and that they can be strong and go without food.

Most Muslims fast except for the old or sick, young children and women who are having babies.

When the next new moon is seen, Ramadan is over, and Id begins.

" During Ramadan, lots of food markets open in the evening. They sell delicious kebabs and naan bread. "

Aasif, aged 9

Getting ready

Families enjoy getting ready for the Id celebrations.

Everyone is busy as the festival of Id gets nearer. Many people like to clean and paint their homes. They hang up decorations like flowers, balloons and streamers and banners that say 'Id Mubarak'.

In Muslim countries markets and shops stay open late in the last weeks of Ramadan.

A Muslim woman buying artificial flowers to decorate her home before Id.

Muslims buy cards and presents, and food for the family feast that takes place when the fast ends.

Malaysians buy food for the Id feast at a busy market.

Families get very excited as they wait to see the new moon so they can start celebrating. Many Muslims call their mosque to find out if the new moon has been seen in the evening sky.

▼

Mosques are places where Muslims meet to study and pray to Allah.

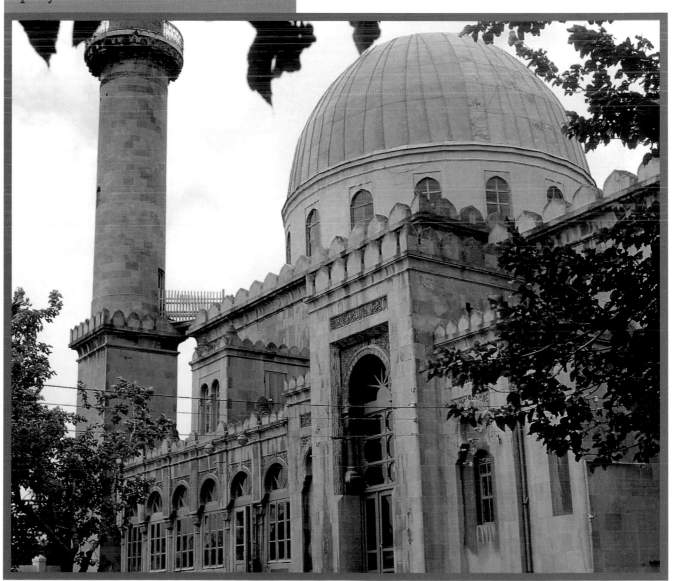

Prayers

Id is a time for prayer and thanksgiving. On the morning of Id, everyone gets up early to go to the mosque for prayers.

Before going into the mosque, people must wash.

Then they go into the prayer hall. The men and boys are in one part, and the women and girls in another.

Mosques are always full and many people pray outside in the courtyard too. In hot countries, Id prayers may be held in a park or a field.

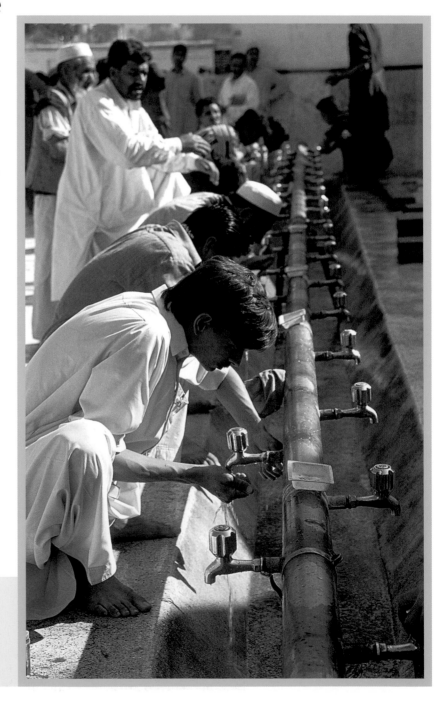

Muslim men wash in a special area before entering the mosque.

The imam leads special prayers at Id. Muslims use prayer mats, and pray facing towards Makkah. This is the city in Saudi Arabia where Prophet Muhammad (pbuh), Islam's last and most important prophet, was born.

" *When we are praying, I stay next to Dad so I can copy what he does.* "
Husain, aged 9

This is a prayer mat that a Muslim might use when travelling. It has a compass so it is easy to find out which way to face Makkah.

Everyone says, "Thank you" to Allah, and asks Him to help them to follow a good Muslim life. Then the imam gives a sermon.

Muslims listen to a sermon for Id in their mosque.

After prayers, everyone goes outside to start celebrating with family and friends.

The Qur'an

The Qur'an is an important part of Ramadan.

The Qur'an is the holy book of Islam. It tells Muslims how Allah wants them to live their lives, and sets out the rules of Islam. During Ramadan and Id, Muslims try to spend lots of time reading the Qur'an.

The Qur'an is written in Arabic. Some people read the Qur'an in their own language, but they try to learn to read it in Arabic too.

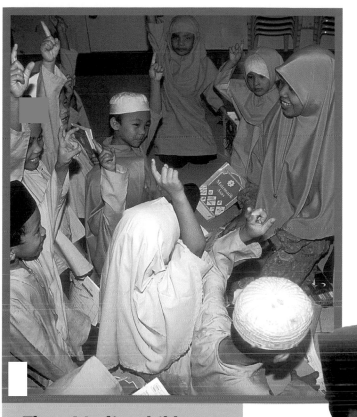

These Muslim children are answering their teacher's questions on the Qur'an.

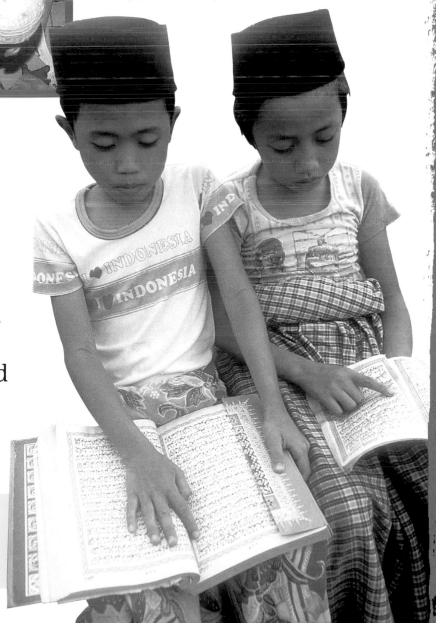

In some countries, such as Malaysia, and countries in East Africa, there are competitions at Id when people stand up and recite parts of the Qur'an that they have learned by heart.

Muslim children learn to read and remember words from the Qur'an.

Sharing and forgiveness

Id is a time for thinking of others.

Muslims believe that Id is a time to be kind to others and to forgive anything people have done to upset you.

They also believe that Id is a time for sharing and giving. They collect money to give to charity so that everyone can enjoy the Id celebrations. This is called Zakat-ul-Fitr.

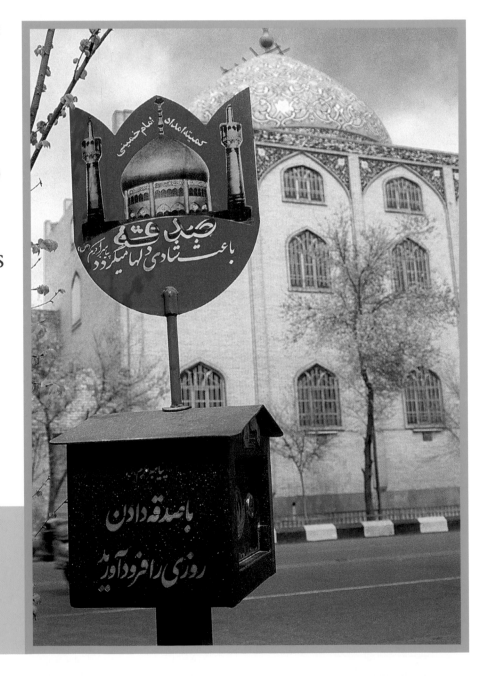

▶ This mosque has a Zakat box, where Muslims can put money in to help the poor.

Muslims try to give the amount of money that would buy a meal for each person in their family.

People give the money before prayers on the morning of Id. Often it is collected at a mosque, so it can be shared out and used to buy meals for the poor at Id.

A Muslim father teaches his son to give Zakat.

66 *My brothers and I all save our pocket money for Zakat at Id. We put it into a big box at the mosque.* 99
Mohammed, aged 9

Children save their pocket money so they can give, too.

Children can use a money box to save for Zakat.

Clothes for Id

On Id morning, families get up early and everyone takes a bath or shower.

Muslims must wash before going to prayer. Many women and men put on a special perfume for Id.

> Perfume is often given as a gift at Id. The Prophet Muhammad (pbuh) liked perfume and encouraged its use.

It is important for Muslims to look their best for the festival. People like to dress up in their best clothes. Some buy new clothes for the celebrations. Men and boys often dress in white, which is the colour of purity.

Muslim women and children dressed for Id.

Many women and girls paint their hands with henna, in pretty patterns called mehndi. This is traditional for special occasions and festivals. Sometimes they buy new jewellery to wear at Id.

" My aunt buys henna to do mehndi at Id. She draws patterns for my sisters and me. "
Fatimah, aged 10

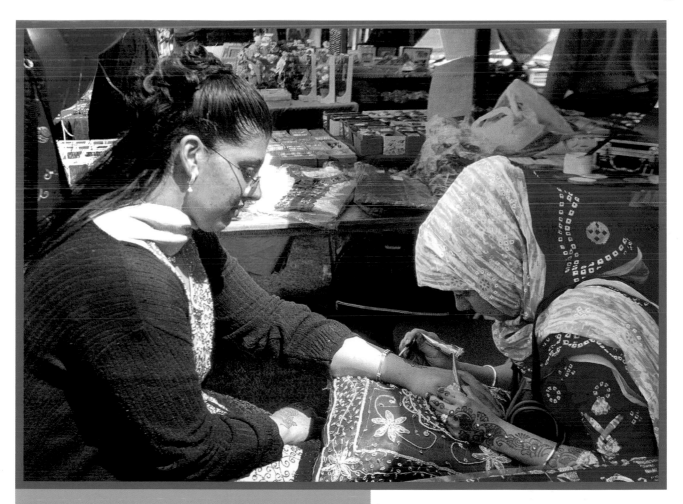

This Muslim woman is having her hands painted for Id at a market.

Cards and gifts

Muslims give cards and gifts to celebrate Id.

These Id cards show pictures of mosques.

In the days before Id, people buy greetings cards wishing 'Id Mubarak' to send to their family and friends.

Children often make their own cards for Id at school.

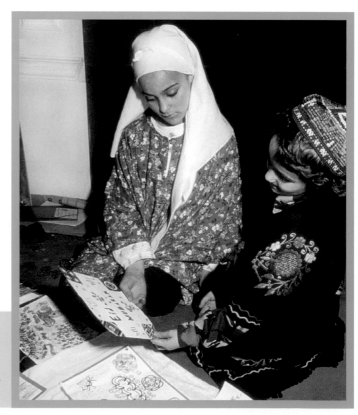

Children may decorate their Id cards with pretty patterns, and sometimes words from the Qur'an.

Many Muslims visit their relatives at Id, after they leave the mosque. The family is important to most Muslims, and relatives like to meet up to celebrate Id as a group.

Families unwrap their presents together. Children may have gifts of new clothes, toys or sweets. They are often given money at Id too.

Grandparents like to give their grandchildren presents at Id.

66 My grandparents give us little bags of sweets at Id. We buy them things for the home like special decorations. 99

Shakil, aged 9

21

Food and family meals

Food is an important part of Id.

On the morning of Id, it is traditional to end the fast of Ramadan with fresh dates and a sweet drink.

Later, families enjoy a big midday dinner. This is the first meal they have eaten in the daytime for a month.

Muslim women in Oman cook a big meal for Id.

22

Sweet foods are popular at Id, like stuffed dates or figs, and spicy puddings made with rice or pasta and sweet milk.

▶ Dishes for Id including sweet milk pudding and dried fruits.

66 *Mum bakes lots of delicious sweets for Id. I like helping her in the kitchen.* 99

Fatimah, aged 10

After the meal, everyone hugs each other three times, as a sign of brotherhood and sisterhood and closeness to each other.

Two sisters hug each other after their family meal at Id. ◀

23

Fun and fairs

Id is celebrated with fairs and street parades.

After the midday dinner, many people like to go out and have fun. In some Muslim countries, there are street parades with people wearing colourful robes and turbans.

These Nigerians are celebrating Id with singing and drumming.

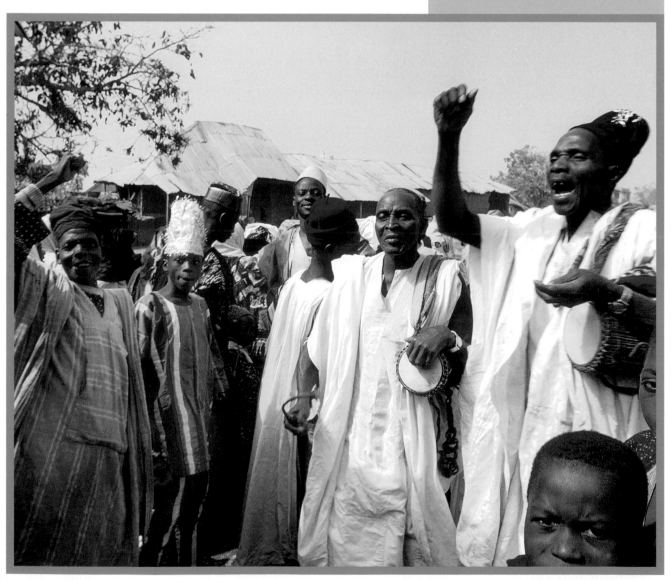

Many cities and towns hold markets and fairs for the festival. There are stalls selling food, sweets, jewellery and gifts, and sometimes funfair rides for children.

British Muslim families enjoy an outing to the park at Id.

" Id is exciting because we get to open our presents, then in the afternoon we all go out to the fair. "
Shaheen, aged 10

There may be actors putting on plays or shows, people playing music and groups of acrobats to watch.

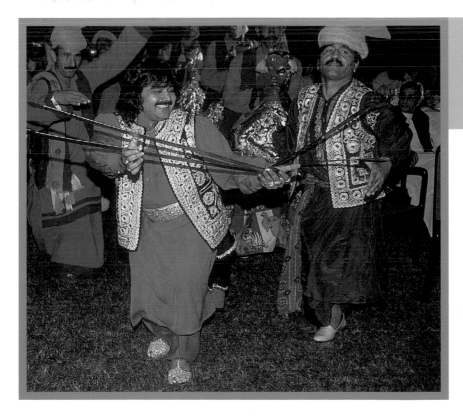

A famous folk artist performs at an Id concert in Pakistan.

Many people also like to hold their own party at Id, and invite all their family and friends.

Sports and games

In Muslim countries, like Saudi Arabia and Algeria, Id-ul-Fitr is a national holiday. Lots of sports events and races are held for the holidays.

Horse racing is popular in North Africa and the Middle East.

" We don't have to go to school at Id. Everyone looks forward to the holiday. "

Abdullah, aged 9

Horse racing is an exciting sport to watch at Id.

There are also camel races in Morocco and Saudi Arabia. Many people travel a long way to bring their camels to race.

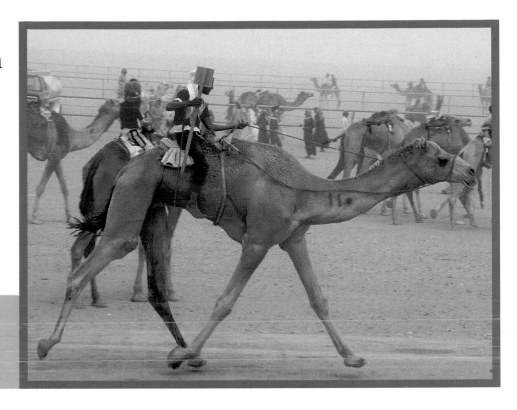

Camel racing during Id celebrations.

Polo is a ball sport played by teams of riders.

In Pakistan and other countries polo is a popular sport to watch at Id. Sometimes tribes or people from different villages compete against each other. They ride horses and sometimes camels.

Glossary

Arabic the language spoken by people living in Arabia, and other countries around the world. It is the language of the Qur'an.

Charity giving money to help people in need.

Imam a person who leads prayers in a mosque and helps Muslims to understand the Qur'an. It means leader.

Islam the religion of Muslims, from Allah, the only creator.

Islamic calendar a calendar that follows the cycle of the moon, unlike a solar calendar which follows the cycle of the sun.

Makkah the city in Saudi Arabia where the Prophet Muhammad (pbuh) was born.

Mosque a place where Muslims go to pray.

Muhammad (pbuh) the final prophet sent by Allah to teach people how to live a good life and worship Him. He lived between 571–632CE.

Polo a ball sport played by people on horses.

Prayer words said when a person asks for Allah's blessings.

Prophet someone chosen by Allah to teach people their religion.

The Qur'an the Muslim holy book.

Ramadan ninth month of the Islamic calendar and the month of fasting.

Sermon (Khutbah) a talk given by the imam before Friday prayer and after Id prayer.

Zakat-ul-Fitr money given to those in need at Id-ul-Fitr.

Islam

Muslims follow a religion called Islam. There are nearly 1,300 million Muslims in the world. Islamic faith begins with the first prophet of Allah, Adam – believed to be the first man on Earth. It was completed with the teachings of the Prophet Muhammad (pbuh), the final messenger of Allah.

Beliefs

Muslims believe in one God, called Allah. They learn about His will through their holy book, the Qur'an. This contains messages that were given to the Prophet Muhammad (pbuh).

Five Pillars

Muslims try to follow the five Pillars of Islam:
1) to state, knowingly and willingly, their belief in one God, called Allah, and affirm the messengership of the Prophet Muhammad (pbuh).
This is called shahddah
2) to pray five times a day
3) to give one fortieth of their savings to the poor
4) to fast for 29/30 days during Ramadan
5) to go, at least once, to Makkah, the city in Saudi Arabia where the Prophet Muhammad (pbuh) was born.

Calendar

Muslims follow the Islamic Lunar calendar, which is a calendar based on the cycle of the moon.

There are six important festivals in the Muslim year. Two were introduced by the Prophet Muhammad (pbuh), and four celebrate events in his life. Id means 'happiness' in the Arabic language, and Id-ul-Fitr is one of the happiest festivals in the Muslim year.

Index